WHEN YOUR SKY
RUNS INTO MINE

WHEN YOUR SKY RUNS INTO MINE

Rooja Mohassessy

ELIXIR PRESS

DENVER, COLORADO

WHEN YOUR SKY RUNS INTO MINE. Copyright © 2023 by Rooja Mohassessy.
First published by Elixir Press, Denver, Colorado.

Designed by Steven Seighman

ISBN: 978-1-932-41881-1

Library of Congress Cataloging-in-Publication Data

Names: Mohassessy, Rooja, author.
Title: When your sky runs into mine / Rooja Mohassessy.
Description: First edition. | Denver, Colorado : Elixir Press, 2023. |
Summary: "Winner of the Elixir Press Poetry Award"-- Provided by publisher.
Identifiers: LCCN 2022044819 | ISBN 9781932418811 (paperback)
Subjects: LCGFT: Poetry.
Classification: LCC PS3613.O3785 W48 2023 | DDC 811/.6--dc23/eng/20221123
LC record available at https://lccn.loc.gov/2022044819

First Edition: 2023

10   9   8   7   6   5   4   3   2   1

in memory of مادر *Madar, my maternal grandmother*
Medhat Al-Zaman Farid Tehrani 1920-1996

for عمو *Amoo, my uncle*
Bahman Mohassess 1931-2010

and for the women of Iran, its true warriors

CONTENTS

I

Iran Politics in First Grade

The television is louder. Inside it grownups
bang into one another like flies caught
in a flytrap, their mouths agape with static.
Some lean like swallows on a downed
powerline and tug at a rope tied to his neck.
Eventually he will stagger off the pedestal onto grass.

Hijab in Third Grade

It's autumn of 1981. Radiators in the hall
clang in time for a new uniform.
Her mother hands the shop lady a list.
There's no need to undress, she says.
Shaking out a full-length overcoat
she slides the schoolgirl's arms
through both sleeves. Wide hems overhang
the shirred cuffs of her peacock-green peacoat.
In the mirror buttoned up the midline
to the schoolgirl's throat is midnight
falling darkly to her ankles, shunning
her shins.

An opaque cutout of a cloud is folded
into a triangle and cast over her head.
Fingers wedge her bangs under repeatedly,
pleading with stars to retreat and keep
out of sight.

Two stray ends of the night droop aimlessly
at her chest. The lady gathers and ties
them into a double knot, a lock
under the chin. It's time to come to terms
with the dark.

Schoolgirl looks up to give thanks
but the lady has forgotten every shape there is
to a smile.

Before and After the Revolution

In the eighties countless shipments were denied
entry onto our land. I wonder if rubber dildos
still buoy on the gray sea, bloated, greasy with the surplus
of embargoed oil, choking that long-inflamed passage
through the strait neck of Hormuz
like a midnight belch. They turned away
many goods and colors, our men,
barely managing, fumbling
to keep our confounding thighs, our unruly hair
out of view and rule the country with a fist,
without aid, trade, or imported hair spray.

The fifties and sixties had ushered in the tango,
the twist would arrive next in cassette tapes
packed with overlap miniskirts. After the revolution,
Sony players still sucked the Hollywood VHS
in place, coached folks in the new Occidental moves.
My aunt shows me a photograph of women
clapping to each other's jig, her belly-dancing
hips swaying in the warmth of a kerosene heater.

By late eighties, the definition of *Dirty Dancing* grows
so broad as to embrace lashes, lips,
and other indecencies. Young women are urged
to keep still, not fiddle with their faces. Then stoning
comes in vogue. Most, me included, miss out
entirely on Swayze's steps. Some friends of friends
get ninety-nine lashes for playing
the clandestine soundtrack past earshot, one lash
for every name of God. Virgins get it the hardest—
guards insert *Coca-Cola* bottles
into rectums. Determined to seal each fate beyond repair,

they take pains to leave vaginas gaping in their wake.
The girls dare not leave their cells, their souls splayed,
pronounced no longer fit to pass
through Heaven's narrow gate.

After half a century, they still won't trust us
with a casual glance, a dildo, though we can't help
but sit with our hair by the window and enjoy
the Persian rose, the scent wafting in,
                    out and in,
                              freely.

Death Was Like a Desire

The advent of the gauze cape and black turban
signaled the growing list of God's mandates.

The gentle nudge under the chin that coaxed us
to look up from our troubles, from dallying

in nothing, no longer sufficed. We must have
been that steeped in sin. We'd raise our heads

in praise of the blended colors of dawn, pull
our chadors over our heads without a second thought,

cup our hands before us, true, we asked mostly
for the cup to pass from us, yet we kissed the cubed dirt

of Karbala and sipped on misfortune. We knew
no doubt we were undeserving—were taught

as much at school and for half a century prior.
But we thought bitterness a remedy, a requisite part

of the cure, we thought it an advance toward a generous
plan, hatching above out of pity if not love, to secure

our spot in heaven. We cried *Allahu Akbar!* hope
streaking our bleak skies. Then the black cloth

appeared, yards suspended from the coatrack, determined
to accompany us out of doors. Like our own guilty

shadows we could not shake, it fell before us
at doorways, denying us access into yet one more room.

It tugged at the back, felt our shoulders and trailed
as in the wake of a casket, the pall dragged underfoot,

muddied in the stampede of a martyred saint. Grudgingly,
we learned to pull it about us, hold it in place, in fear

of new edicts. Fatwas condoned our arrest for the rouged
contours of our lips, not what came out of them, our hands,

the shade of polish on our nails, not who we'd caressed
the night past. In the cell we sat swathed in our last

layer of protection, prayed for lenience, for the whip
to thrash us over, not under our chadors. They said a bare square

inch of our calves, our song, called for repentance. And so
they defiled us at night since, they said, we were dirty already.

War

Iran-Iraq War, 1980-1988

War tricked us into believing it wouldn't stay
while draining from its corner seat
my father's middleclass pockets, gorging itself
on our food and my mother, not unlike our allies
who bled the oil fields of Ahvaz.

*

Once a month our faux-Baroque table stretched
with Ash Reshteh, sturgeon, Sabzi Polo.
Basmati kernels, steamed to utmost reach,
lay pearled and piled in a high-Qajar mound
of aristocracy. Its saffroned crown diffused
a genteel glow into the room, heedless,
like my mother, of the setting sun, unwitting
of yesterday, of where we'd hunched without
power, of tomorrow, our fumbling for the wick.

My mother, mute as a 1920's flower, deaf
as if by grace to the air raid siren, turned now
a blind eye to the thinning leaves of the rationed
book of vouchers war had slipped into the drawer.
A plastic peony pinned high above her right clavicle
caressed her rouged cheek, whispered into her ear.
With a dreamy face swiveling like a doll's,
she greeted guests and looped through folding stools,
her gold hoops lost in her curls. Once a month she'd tuck
the good-sized deaf and dumb society of Tehran
into our three-bedroom flat she'd decked
into a close semblance of a French brothel.

Barefooted children ran to hide and seek, their heads
poking from behind the sprawling imitation
Louis-the-fourteenth armchairs.

*

The evenings, quiet but for guttural cries
torn out of cleft throats, and the play-laughter
of children, eluded the Morality police.
The bane of their lives had turned wartime boon—
not called to the frontlines the deaf signed
into the night sharing what they'd culled
from pictures of martyrs in papers, from a cousin
who both heard and signed, from the muted
television set in the parlor that crawled with foot soldiers,
mullahs, then soldiers again, against a semi-arid
desert backdrop punctuated with explosions,
the close-up wailing of a mother pounding her head.

Though not spared, the war escaped the deaf.
Not because their young children couldn't relay
the twisted turn in the mullah's Friday sermon,
nor because they had never heard the pained midnight
howl of a siren. True, they were immune to the allure
of propaganda, but that wasn't it either.
The deaf were the lamb of God, mild and mute,
and the war loud, too grotesque to fathom.

Yet with guesswork they filled in the missing pieces
into a pastiche of a world view—a circle and a half
about the head for a turban and a dab at the breast
pocket branded the mullahs as thieves. Four fingers
held high over the brow fanned out the full
dynastic plumage of the Shah, and bobbing both hands
up and down in the air dubbed him a puppet.

Then two smacking gestures in midair for stars
and a pointed index meant America was to blame.

*

Then my parents quarreled. I stared at the corner
and accused war of stealing my feline bottle
of *Coca-Cola,* my Friday drink, the skewer
of dripping mutton, the coals cold, my mother
no longer squatting in a flower housedress,
fanning the flames, fanning herself.

*

Then it got bad. I begged war to drown
her gnarled screams and rush us underground
in respite where she rocked me like an infant
before the neighbors. Blind as mice, we kept
to shadows and those among us who could hear
listened for the bomber crossing our heads.

They Were Blind and Mad, Some of Them Were Laughing. There Was Nobody to Lead the Blind People.

Chemical warfare is child friendly
smelling of sweet apples,
                geraniums,

fresh mustard fields mowed at blooming stage,
chlorine—the conflicted scent
                of humanitarian aid
                that cleans and kills as needed,
then there's garlic,
and sometimes something rotten
                like trash.
At times the formula even amuses, froths in spite

of itself into unrestrained laughter
                like a nightmare,
and at room temperature before we enter

                to meddle,
                it's quite airy.
Though heavy and flesh-soluble,
it's chaste, odor-and-colorless.
We add our touch, a favorite flavor, the missing colorant.
Take the vesicant mustard gas—
the poor man's method of reprimand,

                to blind and blister,
                beyond recognition

a shoulder-to-shoulder wave of sons of mothers—
        the older brother,
        middle nephew,
        a first-born only just engaged
        to his second cousin, his first love,
        a father, his next child
        on the way, the newly wedded groom—
        a male pride,

culled from near and far villages,
advancing for the love of God. And it won't be
shy tufts of downy beards,
but their zealous cries that break

the suction seals, fog
the gas masks, tawny mist blearing their sight,
        acid dissolving eyelids.

O the sinful day we meted out poison, sugarcoated in a bright cloud
of mustard flowers—
        promise of savior mounting
        to heaven with every petal.
The gas won't degrade for a hundred years

as the child faithfully lugs
our self-loathing. Unwittingly,
we make of him an aberration,

        alter his genes,
        fumigate his fatigues,
        yellow poison
        seeps like stealth into fat,
        shredding his chromosomes.

Degraded in our own image then,
we caress him tethered to catheters
and nasal cannula.

Who now shall lead the blind with blistered eyes
through barbed-wired lands

      where the leopard refuses
      to lie beside the young goat?

O mothers!
      Come take back your mangled sons
      from the fields. They have lost
      their way to you.

Spared

To create a little flower is the labor of ages.
    —William Blake

Even the outage is for our benefit. They cut
the lights to ease our lives, hide the dread
that betrays us to the children. We burrow
into dark, leave no sign of life above,

block after block deep under
as if we had agreed to be buried. The siren
rushes out of the night, turns the corner
violently past curfew into hollow alleys,

wailing in presage of pending death.
Jostled out of our chores we scramble
for each other, children still curled
over tomorrow's schoolwork quickly smother

the discreet flames of oil lamps, dying
smoke shadows them down the stairwell,
a prayer on every lip. Yet for all its concern,
the siren cannot talk us out of our illusions—

carrying on in basements, we recount
those lies that comfort us, that children smile
for a reason, that the smell of fresh-baked
lavash and the break of dawn are inseparable.

With the first light we emerge into
the aftermath, trace the bomber's path
to the razed intersection, we measure
there the neighbor's catastrophe—

the circumference of her wound, the number
of orphans and their limbs, the depth
of her grief and the blast crater. We talk of stockpiling
potatoes, though it's a sin to be so frightened.

*

At sunset, a child recites an extra surah,
ends the Maghrib prayer with a supplication.
She's thorough, omits no name,
lest they be not spared—

madar joon
mamman joon
baaba joon
leyla joon
khanoom joon
khaleh joon
amoo joon
taran joon
ghazaal joon
aziz joon…aziz joon

Khorramshahr, 1980

In memoriam, Mohammad Hossein Fahmideh

We were soft-fed the sweet dirt of our homeland,
each day some new blessings of war.
    Husband, I tipped that olive beret over your hazel eyes,
    dazzled by the trappings of war.
                May this embroidered tulip keep you, I prayed,
                stitching God Ⓤ to your chest—
                four double-edged crescent swords
                soldered to a dagger—the flower weapons of war.
Once you left us, our son flushed as a redbud,
his temples wrapped in a green headband,
    stood shoulder to shoulder with his friend
    and recited for me his lessons of war.
                Remember how they'd chase that ball
                past twilight?
Now here they sit after school, cross-legged
on the Tabrizi rug, bowing with the teardrop medallions
under the naked bulb—
    they rock to and fro,
    their voices broken with the sweet cadence of surahs,
    our home, husband, is a nest for amorous nestlings of war.
They begged me to string their plastic keys to paradise,
                With this we'll hold fast to the rope of Hossein,
                they swore,
                The Imam says we the children
                are the angel-caresses of war.
How I snapped that day, *You are thirteen!* I cried, *too young to be drafted!*
O they cooed that old love song, a knife in my ear,
                Beheaded,
                trampled
                grandson lamb of the prophet,

we long to be his rose essence of war.
In the doorway, I held the holy book over their heads,
they passed under three times,
> rose to their toes, kissed the golden spine,
> they promised to hold ajar the gates of heaven for me,
>> *O husband, look for them*
>> *at the frontlines, dear God,*
>> *watch over my adolescents of war.*

On a clear Thursday, Mohammad Fahmideh wrapped his body in a shroud
of grenades, and cried,
>> *O God, pull the pins, roll me down*
>> *these green hills of Khorramshahr!*
Husband, won't you come home now? In the courtyard,
>> a lone mourning dove now sings of war.

War of the Cities

It's 1983. Flowers smell of salt
and ashes and *War of the Cities* is intent
on shaking us like dust off the face
of the map, burying us where we hunch
at the kitchen table over tomorrow's schoolwork,
my sister worried the trembling
flame of the oil lamp could give us away.

We wear our day clothes to bed
like soldiers, lie semi-propped up, a flashlight
sinks into Leyla's pillow like a doll, deaf
and dumb, our parents move blindly
about the house, what senses they have,
honed, the sky overhead resigned. Starless.

In the small hours—I daydream
of heaven—Mamman, Baba with Leyla,
my palm in Madar's, we rise
out of an immaculate ruin, against a backdrop
of hellfire, flanked on both sides
by fallen martyrs, their blood scabbed into fields
of poetic poppies that die
at the vanishing point. I run ahead and call capriciously,

Mamman!

She swivels for me like a sunflower, my mute father
whispers into her ear something in passing, something
unassuming yet his voice catches
on a Caspian sea breeze and carries.

The siren means we have four minutes
to spare. I have learned to hear past
the insistent holler. I listen for the seething
stealth that precedes the blast, for the hiss
of a viper close to release of venom.

On his run the bomber favors
densely populated quarters and hospitals.
But why, I wonder, does he always arrive
after dark?

Believers

for Fariba

When he said,
*they're deaf, dumb
and blind so they will not return,*

God meant had we died
in her arms,
            my mother would've carried on

spoon-feeding until certain

we were safely enshrined,
            our halos on exhibit.

Nor did she turn to salt—
even now she looks back though unsure

of what exactly was looted the year the milk

of the rubber tree on the back porch dried up.
She couldn't hear but they carried away

            the grating rattle of her pots,
            giggles that died
            at dinner. Hunger

stayed and reached with our thin manacled mouths

for rationed wafers that perched

higher on the shelf where nothing

wished to be disturbed.

It wasn't like an earthquake—

my mother couldn't hear the night sky
        rip into starry strips,
        she felt the warheads rumble,
        listened with her feet
she kept flat under the table.

With two gold bangles chiming
on each of our wrists and the double-strand
        of jasmine wilting on our chests

my mother had meant to say

        we were believers
        though she'd never read the Qur'an
        nor heard the azan.

By Age Ten I Understood the Heft of Fabrics

and the significance of black after the revolution.
I had no way to know what to feel
about the woman folded inside

those cascading yards of darkness
that transported her like a deluge
down the sidewalks of Tehran,

the hem kicked up, flourishing with dirty spray.
With every step the sharp edge
of a handbag, her elbow jutted at a sudden angle

like a hooded blade. We raised the arms
of our navy manteaux to guide the passing
breeze to our armpits and watched

the chador prevail, overlapped under the chin,
the obsidian length falling weighted like the curtain
that segregated sexes at weddings.

At noon, where we wilted in queue for a cool bottle
of *Coke*, inching our way toward the shade
of the shop awning, the chador shone unruffled,

brilliant with the synthetic glare of a raven.
If a man brushed past it hid one eye, both lips
at a crooked angle; we'd eat our words

midsentence and stare, our parents
jerking us away, worried we'd fall
into a harm worse than a manhole,

a wrong even they could not save us from.
From behind, the sole seam receded askance,
like pursed lips, the hem furtive, not flaring,

not the petal-stitched handsewn fringe
of a homemade chador, the awkward
half-circle stamped with flowers,

but sudden in its zeal, the surreptitious weed
had now appeared, as in Solomon's
temple, fully fledged, too deep to uproot.

At home we played dress up, sashayed
from parlor to kitchen, pulling the coy cloth
over our heads. It slipped like a caress, exciting

our hair with static. I'd almost outgrown
my favorite—covered in lilies, it hovered
a full foot from the floor like an angel

and kept still as I bowed to kiss, then touch
my brow to the fragrant clay of Karbala.

Intoxicated by Verses

Even the Farsi translation, the barely legible
print beneath each calligraphed line calls
for translation. How scholarly she is at ten,
squatting cross-legged, hunched over
the book of spells she spreads daily on her knees.

Thou shalt not touch the verses.

With the full length of her arm she turns
each page from one corner of the magic world
to the next, careful not to scare the sacred,
the gilded accents, little blades suspended,
twinkling over the cursive script.

Thou shalt not recite in a foreign tongue.

She loves the Arab tongue of God, she loves her lips
sliced with surahs, the consonants he thrusts
to the back of her throat, the long vowels
he sustains on her breath. Her incantations soar,
her white chador a floating tent sown

sunny with daisies beaming with childhood.
She pauses to drink at the turquoise bank:
the hand-painted margin of the page hems
her faith and brims with embossed blossoms.

Then dervishlike, rocking with each sibylline verse
that rises out of her pliant throat, she is the reverberating
masjid dome, poised over her paisley janamaz,
birds of praise come nesting,
they come cooing, darting out and into her chador.

Each surah, the utterly incomprehensible
spell she incants from her proud minaret, her cupped hands
an invitation for God to join her, dance
with her on the naked waters of her childhood.
Before long, dancing, too, shall be forbidden.

Ramazan in Tajrish

for Madar

You nudged me with a whisper
to rise an hour before azan
from under the thick of dove
feathers warm with your love
for God and me, the musty grandchild
who had rushed the weekdays
to arrive at you and you were already more
in love and old like walnut trees.

Little did I understand of the hours
past the shuffle of shadows,
why they felt solicitous, safe
only at your home, like uncles
who dropped their manliness
at your door, removed their shoes and stooped
through the narrow frame to greet you.

Whether I hurried out of your bed to meet God
at my paisley prayer mat—the cotton janamaz
you hemmed by hand—or to putter after you
out and into sunlit rooms was moot.

Little did I understand of the prayer
in your gait. For the faint, dehydrated child
the afternoon hours ran from the setting sun
while your white chador shifted faithfully
about you, sprinkled with flowers, deferential
with the remaining minutes.

Though too young to fast, even then
I knew, when I pestered you
with a ten-year-old's dogged demands,
to rouse me for Sahari—the day-old lavash we tore
like a promise between us, buttered at near dawn,
and to keep our secret from Mamman and Baba,

I knew in your low-cloud voice
that would nudge my sleeping cheek only once,
Did you think I would not hear you?
in the reluctance of it lodged the caress
of those childhood days.

Madar

Some Thursdays she climbed down the arched foot
of Alborz where the northern flank of the city
wrestled its way up the quiet of snow-covered slopes.

The busy leaves of her chador rushed
to her feet alternating in the burnished shades
of autumn and bare sycamores reached over her veiled
head with their age-old limbs. She'd cry,

سید خندان!
Seyed Khandan!

into lowered windows at a hairpin
curve where the rush hour slackened,
the neat autumn leaves about her face
scattered at the repeated gust

of greasy air. Like a pigeon weaving
through the grey lawlessness of exhaust
and people she'd scurry for the neon yellow Peykan
that had harkened to her trilling call—the battered

communal cab would ferry her across town to us,
the backseat already spilling with elbows,
forearms and bundles. Her lips would quiver
with the ninety-nine names of God, her fingers

would nudge, nudge along the rounded beads
till she'd arrived at our overhead bridge.
Each Thursday, chockful of stories and poems,

I hurried to find her at the kitchen table
like a present only just unwrapped,
the leaves a heap of fall color at her feet.

مادر!

Madar!

I'd cry,
as though invoking the one hundredth name of God.

Childhood

Juliet, the dice was loaded from the start.
　　—Mark Knopfler

Frightened, my childhood refused
to attend my life,
though I invited it repeatedly.
Shy and broken,
it handed me shards I dusted off,
demonstrating how
to assess the depth
before easing into pain.

I blew on its sore eyes,
resorted to lies. *Your desk*, I said,
and the imploded
hole to your right,
on the cross-taped window,
will still be here,
sparkling
like the stars above
when you return.
Meanwhile, I promised, *I'll continue*
to search for the bullet
lost in the house.

II

The Immigrant Leaving Home and Guilt

I kept both near—the miniature Qur'an of Madar,
and ameh's letter, the sentient talisman, suffused
with the power of a Matriarch in the making.
For years I'd slip it out of the frayed envelope
and gauge how far I'd strayed. Like hot iron
branding a lamb she'd left her mark, the choke
collar yanked ardently one last time, one more
fledgling to leave the brood for good now.

I ponder still, awed at ameh N.'s methods,
her noblesse of motif. Fortysomething and handsome,
a chemist and communist, she pressed gingerly
as into a bruise, conjured nuanced variations
of heartbreak—what was to become in my absence
of those helpless at home, she wrote—Mamman lost in
the foyer, oblivious to the wail of the siren that rushed
neighbors to safety, deaf and dumb dear Baba,
what of him rooted at dusk under the sagging fall
canopy of the persimmon, his child-interpreter gone
for good, her heavy schoolbag no longer in need
of shouldering. Our home handicapped,
forever forlorn as Mrs. Havisham's.

Midway, a lyric by my beloved Hafez, a couplet embedded
strategically—her suave hand reaching out with rose
candy, and the Avesta of Zarathustra—the yardstick
she'd bid me align my actions with, in the dissolute land
of exile. Last came the finale, gushing in the fervor
of a sermon, her voice old, thick as blood, the West woven
in rhetoric of temptation. O how those lines tug still
at my denim miniskirt each time I make to take my seat.

O how her metaphors bore that day like fallout
into an unequipped prepubescent body, a mined
battlefield, yelping, yelping with contusions.

دوستت دارم،
Doostet daram, she'd closed with.

A hunched bundle airlifted out of devastation,
hauled in mercy across a continent, I sat buckled
into my seat reading and rereading my love letter.

The Immigrant and Skin

We'd landed, and on our way
to the terminal I lost myself
to a foulard. It toyed
in the lenient light of the bus with garden green,
then chartreuse; it made no qualms,
draped no part
of the young woman in order or out
of deference.
No proper plan
in particular.

I watched
it dip into her cleavage, gradually slip
off the curb of one shoulder as though teased
by the jolts on the road.

She'd left her throat bare, unaware
of the tiny tremors rolling
with the sip
of *Evian*,
and the moist syllables that cohered, her breath there,
very near her travel companion.

We were many,
our long-censored eyes now privy
to titillation and play.
I, the prepubescent voyeuse,
transported by the rippling, the recline
of her head, tugged as if in jest
by the whorled ends—a tight crowd
mingling in the small of her back.

I watched the lovers' heads—dovetailed, a dome
sparkling by the window like the shrine
of Imam Reza in Mashhad.

Then the noise that pealed
from the forward thrust of her throat
and ceased, her rouged mouth delayed,
tilted like a goldfish come to feed.

A mouth like that would've been taped back home
I had no doubt, without questioning, with or without lipstick.
I reached for the nape
of my neck, pared by the open air.

The Immigrant and Envy

In the Getty version her legs are crossed,
the gossamer cloth pressed
into her pubis. In an instant she'll withdraw
her palm and recline onto the sham.
Ribbons of gold shimmy about like wild fringes
on a flapper girl. In Rembrandt's rendering a putto
vibrates by the bedpost, the velvet canopy sagging
in excess like the amazon-green drapes
Miss O'Hara fashioned into a dress.

The brazen subterranean tower ablaze,
O so blinding.

*

I only understood Scarlett
two-thirds in when she got down digging
for frozen roots, the grit of war
caked into her nails, her faded affairs
and frilly gowns trailing like bait
from page to page. I skimmed the Civil War
that dragged endlessly like exhortations
of the Mullahs back home, but I strained
over Rembrandt's Danaë. I understood God,
dry light at Asr prayer pouring
onto my janamaz. I understood shavings of the sun,
the forked sword of the prophet sharpened
on the great ingot of gold,
sparks shooting vigilant, but I couldn't
conjure the cry, the throat that seemed to yield
to bliss like a genie released at last, the rose-blossom
of health and cellulite rippling

warm as raw fleece, the half-lifted rump, a pale linen
bunched in the damp of it.

I harkened to the picturesque call of maidens
from tower tops, the clichéd cry of the fallen
from grace. I could even fathom the tear
of pubescent girl flesh
in the solitary cells of Evin prison,
but Rembrandt's Danaë!
How he wished for her thighs to do more
than acquiesce. Where she'd found the aplomb to bare more
than one length of skin at a time
I had yet to learn.

The Immigrant and Lament

Here's how it went—
the wind soughed,
I played deaf and stared
ahead those mornings the sky
was a clear-day blue.
I was busy, had begun already

to flay my skin. Yes, it hurt.
How to tell it so you'd understand I didn't like
the feel of it anymore, nor the flesh
and blood I'd brought with.
Well, I had nowhere to turn. I'd clambered out
of rubble and ran
for you, you see. Then, pared,

I began nitpicking, (it would be years
before a variation of my smile
or gait would scab with an inflection
I thought you'd approve). I picked till then
at my insistent face in the mirror, bridled
my mother tongue, swallowed radifs and quatrains.
Once obsolete, I could lie
about where I'd come from and those
I'd left to die.

I stood sorely out of doors, blended
with hollow berries
and poisonous bristles of the common yew.

Don't get me wrong. None of it was your fault.
It wouldn't have mattered if I'd been a guest.
It wouldn't have mattered. If I'd been a guest

I would've known my place.
I would've arrived with my very tongue and God,
cupping a bowl of night-blooming jasmine
in my palms, the troop of sitar players
at my heels would've set the mood at the moonlit
divan and the arm's length between us
would've been fragrant with petals.

But fear trembled
in the tenor of my voice and settled
into the carriage of your mouth.

Rose D'Ispahan

I always visit the same spots at the Huntington
Botanical Gardens. On the path to the Chinese pavilion,
I turn the corner at Shakespeare's bust, past the small
fountain neatly spilling. Advanced in midsummer,
the garden's flooded with profuse personalities—

> *Ingrid Bergman,*
> *American Beauty,*
> *Abby's Angel.*

I pause at *la rose du petit prince,* bent low
to the ground, the silken hem of her mauve petals
scalloped like an old nightgown—a pale ghost
of the early days where she stood aloft the escarpment,
brandishing her four thorns, coughing her low-throated
cough into the wind, like the husky sounds
from your then lush lips no one suspected
mute till parted. I try to remember why I liked her
best, not because le *petit prince* left, as princes must.
I envisage the end—the rose chilled
without her screen. Without her glass globe
the drawn-out draft pulls at her limbs, she succumbs
to frost, the butterflies called away. Now splayed
at my feet, uprooted, fallen from the twinkle-star,
she has yet to recover. Mother, you
were such a proud flower. You packed for me
knowing it was for good. You never asked,

> *Who now will hear the phone ring?*
> *Who is to interpret this lingering ache?*
> *Who will tell of the news, the war, who?*
> *Who will sign for the mouths in constant motion?*

Mother, once your little prince left, how did you haggle
for rationed coupons? Who signed the air-raid siren
into your eyes? You managed though the house no longer heard
the doorbell, could barely read or write, every room dumb,
half-opened doors shutting without a sound.

I tried to imagine you dying in different ways,
but you lay unconscious again, caught under the fridge,
its heavy door yanked off, the light inside flickering
its last. Once I dreamt you on your back,
someone had pulled the wall-size canvas of the English colonel
in the hall over you like a full-length shroud.
At the airport, you remembered the head buried
in you breast was only a child's.

خدا نگهت داره،

you signed through my tears.

*

I rise, having paid my respects as though you were dead,
and continue on my path to the pavilion, searching still
for *rose d'isphahan*, the pompon of Princes.
You tamed me Mother, you have a prince's promise,
I will be forever responsible for my rose.

At Twelve

for Amoo

I learned to treat it with reverence
when it began to arrive with less
then less frequency, the small
sea-blue tin box casually wrapped
in translucent wax paper,
cross-tied with white cotton twine,
the gray lead seal guarding it

like a coffer of family treasures.
It sat far back on the top shelf
where it's cooler, barricaded
by tall jars of your strawberry jam
and *Belpaese* stacked on top
of *Pecorino*, the wrapper left open
to breathe like an unbuttoned silk blouse.

You gingerly minced parsley,
soft-boiled eggs and the heart of an onion,
like the paint you daily primed on your palette.
The condiments and the stacked pyramid
of buttered toast were solely for my pleasure,
you courted only that tiny glass
I filled faithfully—the Russian bottle

in the icebox, sweating and expectant,
would freeze-cleave to my hand and rush
for your glass, fuming like a captured spirit.
Your eyes blue as mischievous flames.

Girded with a rose rubber band, the round tin
lay sealed on the table, each ovum
vacuum-pressed into the other in the damp
brine, waiting for release like puberty.
You snipped the band gritty with salt,
gently tapped the box on its head
as though asking for permission to enter,
before slipping the top off.
The moist content cohered,

suspended an inch over blue
like dense fog over the Caspian—
a silver cloud of roe condensed in midair,
glistening, bronzed as the Roman statues
of *Galleria Borghese*. With a silver spoon
you scooped a careful amount,
raised your glass to the harbinger friend

who could still come and go across the sea
bearing gifts without risking jail time,
and to the proud fish with the uplifted nose,
upheaved and harvested at twelve,
a strip of snow-white mountain chain
stretching the length of her body
from gill to tail, whose fifteen kilos
of hospitality, the largesse of her white belly
made us bashful as we sat before our one
ounce of homeland. Thankful it had escaped

confiscation at the airport, we counted
every grain popping in our mouths,
running out like luck.

As the sea closed her fecund womb
to mark the start of life in exile,
I'd washed ashore far to the west,
about to drop my first egg into your hands.

Silence

Your mouth was not always song. It was the living room
cracked wide into a tilted ravine
where you flew and I sat in the deep and nodded as needed
in our near conversations,

or it was the taxi cab, the museum,
twisted in another visit into a sudden maze irreparable
when inspired by a nude bronze, you were reminded
of the time Poseidon punished
Odysseus and I hesitated to ask his crime.

With no points of reference, I created my own.

You planted no solicitous sign posts, nor painted them
pretty for a girl-child. I hung on your French
and Italian words, but you scattered
no bread crumbs to collect,
to arrive safely at you. Bird omniscient!
When you soared over our ravine you
cast no shade and I was old enough
to make you coffee, old enough to need
a bra, but when you recounted stories,

no, it was all too late for lullabies, you omitted determiners,
the demonstrative pronouns
went missing and I rummaged, rummaged
through, yet could not fit
your gorgeous adjectives, the adverbs refused to fall
into place in my jigsaw puzzle.
They sat in my inept hands
like wasted love. I wanted to love
Poseidon at the fountain, Odysseus,

Picasso entertaining the Parisians at Montparnasse.
I was shy for hyperbole but before we met
I had early memorized the morning star—
a short while ago I could easily forget
my name. Before we met to spend evenings
in your living room, live in hotel rooms
where fresh-cut flowers never died
and I prayed no one would address
the question that followed to me.

But I was in it for the long haul.
I ate at your splendid table, adorned it daily
with a stem from your garden and memorized
the undulations of your love. The often whip
and always caress of it censored, modeled
my becoming. And I was
to your liking. Master sculptor, when you pressed
upon me I fed you spoonfuls
of silence, the salve for the lacerations in your mouth.

Ferrara

I have shown you this much—Rome and these wide
avenues where bicycles catch in furrows, their bells breaking
the repose of pale afternoons. You studied the grand
Northern town from a corner of yourself,

with the same wide-eyed look I'd seen you leaf through
the glossy book of Roman nudes on my coffee table.
Each time we came around a bend, you searched
for footing in a pigeon at a piazza, the gypsy who offered

you roses. Our detour led us to the house of Este,
its façade of pyramids imposing on the air. At twelve,
you still outgrew the shoes I bought though your visage
was a kaleidoscope, shards early settled into a design, resigned

and taciturn. Inside the Pinacoteca you stood your ground,
not shirking the forceful strokes, the thick grease of aged
patina: you said you understood the master had tarried
for no one, the smears of paint glossy-wet as if only yesterday

the sure hand had rubbed the sluggish brush
onto a profile to highlight an unnegotiable truth. I knew
in time you'd learn what it meant to be a man, love men
as I did, their desire and the give of a canvas. I knew

turpentine burned the back of your throat at night.
That evening, we dined at the pensione. Squid ink dyed
the seam of your lips and I pocketed a lacquered
spoon to amuse you, fed you the rest of the myth

of Eurydice, all to keep from you that we'd forsaken
our loved ones and soon we'd outstay our welcome here.

Like a Rosebud

She chose a red-sherry chiffon dress even the wind
had no hold to, sheer in the light, flurried
with small polka dots, trifling with childhood.

Her reflection reached to fill the full-length mirror.
She was done growing yet I couldn't fathom
what she'd do if someone approached to kiss her.

She pulled the sash to the front, looping it into a neat
double bow. The slit sleeves fell away, elbows poking,
her narrow hips thrust forward like a boy-child

careful to piss away from his pants. Gangly
in the petite dress, she turned and asked how she looked.
Her arms dangled, fingers almost to her knees.

I said she could get measured now
for the pair of shoes I'd promised, with as much heel
as she pleased now that her feet had fully formed.

At *Bruno's* she picked out a lustrous-red patent lamb hide
and low kitten heels. I matched her dress
with a ruby-red knit tie and took her to dinner. She grew

into a woman, into a fruiting tree, made room for men,
not for the shadows they cast. Years later, she came
home married, sat across the arm of my chair,

and we posed for a photograph, her slender
legs her own, folded like a rosebud.

All About Me

If I sit silently, I have sinned.
    —Mohammad Mossadegh

O my feline soul,
when he asked the child in the front row to tell
all about herself, *tout sur toi,* Monsieur Pichon
couldn't have known she'd chew on the Swiss fountain pen

and draw a blank though she could've told him
he was her favorite, and *les noms de toutes les fleurs,*
colors and every disparate part
of her body she knew to name without checking, the way she knew
her country, the cat hunched unwell on the world map—

she had color-coded the legend enough times, shaded counties
and *fleuves,* she could account for the neighbors, for war
chafing at the pinched throat she'd yet to hear purr,
the inflamed eye—the great lake of Urmia now shrunk
to a pained salt-water slit. She'd traced up the proud swell
of its chest in brown, the western border matted
with the dried blood of boys. O my soul, you shy away
even now, though I catch you glinting in the dark
of my eyes. Had you shone as from a plastic tiara
on her brow, steadied her hand though she slouched
homesick at her desk, she would've scribed then with the flourish
of a Persian calligrapher, a catalogue of herself, warriorlike
she would've guarded to reveal only that
which could be fairly rendered into a foreign tongue, of a profile
in relief, of rivers and veins. She would've begun to relate

to the curious Monsieur Pichon how she had personally seen
the queen back home, occupied with her charge—
a country and its mountain chains, plain as dry bread
but for gorse thriving and dusty butterflies resting
on unmarked trails. She would've illustrated a picture
of herself pressed flat as a papermoon, to make room
for the good shepherd, his flock tumbling along,
dropping little pellets, the green scent of wintering
foothills caught in a cumulous of fleece. Had you been there,

she would've spun in her Baluchi skirt stitched
with mirrors and demi-moons, to show
and tell, and the children would've reached for the shards
of light dancing on the walls, not shunned her like a castaway.
But you, my O young and foolish soul, forgot
your song, your tongue,

without you, the girl waited and in the minute
remaining of the period, she scribbled,

Je ne sais pas qui je suis.

Straniera

two years into exile and still waiting to fall
    into place   feel at home   in a thong   won't venture
        out to where she can't touch
heads to the beach
    daily like homework   wades through a bronzed sea
of bodies splayed   under the late-summer *ferragosto* sun
    pursed at the tips   tanned breasts pull
        languidly to each side
like half-filled leather bags   she looks for an empty patch
of beach the size   of a janamaz spreads the towel lies
        back luxurious bodies
of clouds stretch   in white marble gestures of Venus
    crouching at her bath   she rolls onto
        her belly undoes   the strap pulls
    the bikini top from under   firmly pressing
her breasts into the heat the burn
        of transgression and turns
to bare sandy nipples
to the world though no one   is looking no cup-bearer
        waiting for a sacrificial offering
    of a swim top no Roman rite   of passage to brave
        clouds carry on cut across upstage
    each other   a low one casts   a modest shade
festooned over her like a clean   white chador fetched from a line

First Kiss

I wish someone had explained
how wide to open for that French
kiss, how to keep my front teeth
out of his way, angle my nose,

breathe and let the tip of his tongue
probe like a feeler. I dodged it
to make room, rolled mine
into a morsel, nursed it
inside a cheek and swallowed
my growing need to spit.

If he entered too far I stifled
the gag, when he slid under
I drew back. When he relaxed
it thickened and slugged
in my crammed mouth, sloshing
through the excess saliva. He'd pull
away then quickly resume, kiss me again
and again as though he had yet to get
what he'd come for.

With each brief lull I came up for air,
wiped my mouth and downed the buildup,
the hard taste of liquor laced with the scent
of a day-old ashtray.

I told myself with time
I'll get this, the way I'd learned to swallow
without chewing a tough cut of a sirloin steak.

No, I wish someone had explained this
was an invitation of sorts. I'd been invited
to *la dance des langues*:

I wish he'd curtsied and waited
for the first note, a custom
to commence a *menuet*
á deux *mouvements*.

I wish he'd lingered at my lips,
the rounded doorway,
then bowed a little to enter
and greet *Marguerite,* the pearl
of daisies, damp at dawn,
not a *dent de lion*, a common sedge,
the bucktoothed teen, her breasts
only just budding.

O how I would've looked upon him then,
with my dark eyes.
I would've danced, taken the heat, the burn
of the new day. My mouth young,
O so eager to please.

Sky and Sea

A pair of buoyant thighs
in denim skinnies, held
tightly though impatient
with the lateness of the hour,
or a pair of lips that rarely part,
the lower bruised and azurite,
quivering with restless ripples.

Little keeps them apart
but a shy shade of cyan. To pry
sky from sea you'll need
the Egyptian funerary tool, *Setep,*
for *Opening of the Mouth.*
See, one billows like the blue
gorget of a hummingbird
while the other keeps still
and spreads.

Magnolia Grandiflora

Once I'm tall enough I'll be tutored
by Magnolia Grandiflora and learn to bloom
large in secret places high above the treetops.

In time I'll move on from dearest eglantine,
heart-shaped and neat and roam august—
an Arabian leopard in relaxed, mottled skin.

When I'm tall enough I'll concede and pliant
folds shall part at pressing. I'll refuse to glow
French and velveteen like a boudoir
bedside lamp. With pulsed light I'll flare

for pleasure. I'll paint my lips, withhold
my smile and make fallow expectations bleed,
breed a race of men who make love as friends.

III

I've Asked for it

this is how my flesh is made
taboo—desire bares
its head you beat it
with the same stick your father
raised imagining you differ
from a fanatic who upon seeing
a swallow prays for the cup
to pass from him
he takes no notice
of clouds thin and see-through in the distance
of rarified air
of the respite offered by limbs
bowing under the belly of sparrows

you lower your gaze for fear
of the open sky swallow
a holy verse like a pill
the orgasm though is inevitable
your frame shakes
each spasm a reason
to consign your wife and daughters to a shapeless
corner of the room their hair
tied back out of the wind you cannot help
it jostles its way in clumsily rude as the repressed id
which in spite of all efforts won't learn the difference
between wife daughters and sky
it can't help
but crave the flush of dawn
the swift whip
of the pixie swallow against its cheek
to remedy this you escort me to an improper
room of your dreams

it's all very heady here
I'm a minor or a married woman whose bare arms belong
as yet to no one or someone
in your dream I'm dirty I've asked for it
which is fine but won't you step
into the open won't you
call my name don't you know
here I stand the fresh air this slice of blue
the taste of rapture in my mouth

Loneliness

Here, too, I made my home,
took the gracious bamboo
at face value, the hermaphrodite
papaya trees grew on me—volunteers
pushing through cracks of sidewalks.
The flesh-toned butter of their fruit
I've taken countless times
into my mouth and swallowed
my praise the way one refrains
from flattering a loved one.

I've been familiar with the men
of this land and their jet-black hair,
friendly with women, their thighs
parted in monsoon afternoons,
the air pressing, pregnant with downpour.

I raise my glass to you with both hands,
arms outstretched the way you like it.

You mistook me for a god when the vowels
of your tongue in my mouth
rang near your own, when I learned your cadence
by heart, you thought it effortless like love.

See how far I've journeyed to meet you,
crowned my head with your exotic flowers,
petals furled back obscenely like fanged
creatures. I've been intoxicated numb
by frangipani, by the noxious fumes
of fermented tofu in your alleys.

I am the phoenix, all but infallible,
a dark consort for you, O mighty dragon!
I'm your neighbor from the nearby
land of rose gardens and poems of praise.
I have travelled the silk road, the barbarian
has come empty-handed this time,
a beggar so poor she falls in love
with anything and you are safe
to love. Like a tourist, I adorn myself
with you, we need have no strings attached.
Exile suits me, convenient
as an affair. Kiss me again,
here I rest my head,
longing for a dreamless night.

Godliness

Here is not the peach-domed Turkish bath dappled by holy light, nor a Roman Balneum of blue mures sweating with frescoed flowers. This is Shanghai extravagance—the ancient rituals of purification revamped and commodified under the sky-roof of a 24/7 multi-level neon complex of singing pools, deluxe packages of acupressure and pedicure.

By the foyer, men and women clad in starched pj's gamble at Mahjong, sip on moonshine. Their flushed children gambol on the heated marble floor above; guqin drawls in the quiet room where guests are resting before palm-sized screens clipped to raise-and-recline beds. I'm signed up for the mini-package and sit simmering in the nude, in a jade-tiled pool, watching a crew of migrant middle-aged women in wet uniforms of black lace lingerie and gumboots pass through the fog, call out numbers, hustle with their invisible sleeves rolled up past the elbows. They look wholesome as plain meals, their cheeks ruddy from the furnace heat of twelve-hour shifts, their backs brilliant.

二十二, *Er-Shi-Er!*

A woman hollers my number in the pitch of vendors at wet markets calling on shoppers to collect their plucked and prepared chickens. I carefully step over the slippery lip of the pool and follow. At her table, she plops me down without ado, props my limbs against her own and begins to pummel and knead. From under her blue scouring mitten, dark dregs roll out and away. Her sweat falls on me like rain from a full fleshy cloud. She bastes me with a warm marinade of milk and honey, leaves to return with a hose, rinsing us both down in the cool stream. Then, smiling in her sheer demi-bra and panties, she presses two fingers into my thigh, the flesh rebounds buoyant, my olive skin squeaking pink like new hairless plastic—

I am Venus of Willendorf, reborn into the lean fecundity of the 21st Century!

I say, **谢谢** *Xie Xie*, and attempt with small talk to show off my mastery of the four tonal inflections. She's on a schedule and no, she cannot accept the tip. Yet I wish she would sit down, I'd fan her face, buy her iced jasmine tea. We stand naked and inches apart, our bodies steaming, but before me now appears the gaunt ghost of a younger me. I'm a spoke in the greased immigrant machinery that propels America forward. Down on all fours, in grey sweatpants, a gauze of perspiration glistening on my upper lip, I am bearing down into a woman splayed prone. A cathedral diamond glitters in her palm. Too raised to lay comfortably against the floor mat, she's twisted it in for comfort. I press my double-jointed thumbs into the junction at L-4. When they give I replace them with my elbows. Then I climb onto her upper back, balance my knobby knees on a gnarled knot behind a shoulder blade. From there I pummel the kidney meridian like a boxer who knows the game is lost but puts in a good fight. How willfully they rolled, those knots, for seven long years they resisted my insistence!

Sister,

I look into the flushed face before me and hold her gaze a moment longer.

I know you strain for a living. I know you wish you could fly West, earn more, send money home. I couldn't save any of my fifty dollars-per-hour for the hour that didn't end there. God knows I tried. I can tell you though, sister, about follow-up-phone-calls, about the cultivated consolations I heaved daily from my breast and cooed into the receiver in comfort. One had rested so poorly, the other had suffered a flare up, her intolerance to gluten her nightmare, another couldn't drop the extra pound from the midriff. Sister, you're spared here from flashing that five-dollar-smile that spells out tip. It hurts at the heart, believe me. Here at home, you're responsible only for that first layer of clean dirt that exfoliates with the coaxing of your blue mitten. They don't expect small miracles from you, they don't expect you to melt away calci-

fied errors. You have no need to skirt around the truth, you are not called upon to dissolve a lifetime of errant choices hardened into unyielding pebbles slipping under layers of fat. O sister! I know your gait, the way you shift weight like a beast of burden, but they catch up with us, you see. There I kneaded their bodies, here I teach their young. Go if you must, but here at home, you walk away with your soul to sit at breaktime with your own people.

辛苦了. *Xin Ku Le,* I say instead, and let her shoo me in the direction of the steam room.

辛 *Xin*: assiduous industry, diligence
苦 *Ku*: bitter misery, exhaustion
了 *Le*: action completed.

Mrs. Farahmand and Mrs. Henderson Share Drinks on the Eve of War

The moment you enter I stretch across
my moist lips a taut and glossy smile,
transparent as *Saran Wrap*, preserving us
at a good arm's length where you lean
into my island, your unbuttoned
blouse breathing, your favorite
perfume wafting over.

I realize it's mere temporary mercy,
yet it saves us, believe me, my strained
charade, from spoiling the perfectly blameless
afternoon, our cultural incompetence betraying us both
with such topics as the Red Sox, Axl Rose
and how well he has aged, the toughness of sanctions

on Iran, which member of the female
body is left bare in the Qur'an and whatever
happened to my mother and her tongue.
A long list of taboo topics each petering
out at the embarrassed dead-end,
though a small amount of ill-at-ease
we can both tolerate like a low-grade fever.
From the corner graciously beams
my professional Cuisinart with the continuous feed head,
my gambit for reviving the dead air. The kitchen,
too, I've aired, sumac subdued, cardamom
and clove, saffron, sealed in vials lest they seep

and clash with our summer menu of baby
kale and nasturtium, thin sole
fillets propped up on bouncy beds of greens.

Yet a few cocktails in, we predictably
thaw in our Riviera high chairs, I lean
into the counter and confess how long
it's been since sex, you advise how best
to ease into the full dosage of black cohosh
now that menopause has hit.
Then after a boozy tiramisu we sop up
with a shared spoon, I usher you, Mai Tai in hand,

onto the twilit patio where a phalanx of ghosts
conjured from 500 BC streaks crimson
the California sky—
the Athenian dead,
Darius the Great,
Alexander, Persian warriors, their armors cast aside, stand in line
with those who loved us,
my uncles who died in exile,
their wives alone in hospice. Your dead, too,
whoever they be, stand should to shoulder with mine,
all on the same defeated side.

Glosses worn off, our smiles almost clear
the air now of centuries of mistrust. We've reassured the afternoon
with nods of understanding, dreamt each other
harmless, consoled with dabs of moisturized touches,
and here we sit in the glow of the tired sun, silently sipping
our final drinks. As our countries brace for war my border
of white roses sways before us like a flag of truce. Your gold
highlights toy with the last light, my bone-
white roots call for a touch up and I think
to myself, look how well we managed
against such heavy odds and shed no blood.

Interview for Asylum

after Sylvia Plath

Discarding your hijab is non-negotiable, ma'am.

I've made a note of the signs of torture
on your face but you'll need to hold
in piss till told what's next (*insists the officer*).
Yes, this is a free country,
   (*smiles graciously*)
we are indiscriminate
with positions that indulge our kicks.

In effect, the process is rather involved,
   (*he continues*)
for starts, you'll need to second-guess,
divine a way to ravish.

The nude inside
of a thigh, the front slit
of a skirt will do for openers, though rather common.

You'll need to support yourself
on your arms and keep at it till we come. It won't be long.

Let us examine your profile. Please stand.
   (*scrutinizes her face closely*)
In time, you'll need to carve and discard the inordinate
chunks of your cheeks,
reject the ridges
of your congenital jaw.
   (*returns to his desk*)
Now remember, blow jobs should be airy—

be sure to make room.
As for your blood, it's thick. It extends too far back.

      (*examining the documents*)

                Have you kept a record? No? Drain it then.
                Soon you won't be needing it to draw from.

Please step up on the scale now.
                O how inadequate!
You clearly cannot endure.
Deficient, mal-informed, possibly abused during transport,
almost dark, from some country, dumb, likely slow to come.

              Artlessly insecure!

And your tongue. Utter a few words, would you?
              Discordant. Do you hear it? Can it be tuned?

O so quiet! Terrified beyond despair. She'll never serve.
Send her back. (*the assistant points to a clause in a document*)
              She'll be getting old anyhow.
              There's little we can do for her now.

When Your Sky Runs Into Mine

The curse never fell upon our nation till now! I never felt it till now.
—William Shakespeare

When your sky runs into mine
I'll be sure to see to your needs, address you
with the appropriate personal pronoun.

If you've left behind your *hands, organs,*
dimensions,
senses, affections, passions,
I'll assist you in seeking immunity, in signing
the requisite papers.

When your sky runs into mine
I'll grade your pigmentation by degrees,
screen you under fluorescent glare
and adjust your Protection Factor.

In class, when your child raises his hand
I'll give him a chance
to demonstrate your literacy rate.

In mixed company,
I'll commend your tongue
on how well it speaks my tongue
as you pronounce my name,
your accent on a foreign syllable.

When you Naturalize
I'll welcome you with a handful
of questions:

Where were you born?
Are you still mourning?
Have you sworn
to return home?

When I visit your country
I'll carry a trifle of your words
to use in fair trade. I'll express myself
with a generous tip and thank you
and yours for civilizing your children
not to stare, for sterilizing
the countertops for my intestinal flora.

When your sky runs into mine
I'll read your poem
and compliment Jalal ad-Din Rumi
on his mother tongue.

Sanctions

You're gonna catch a cold from the ice inside your soul.
—C. Perri, D. Lawrence, B. Yeretsian

Mr. president T.,
I'm your Iranian who also believes in a high headcount
of silver canisters to enrich a nation,
in virility spiking
tantamount with stockpiling and hoarding
of sperm or black hornets for instance.

Though all that piling
piling and abstaining
proliferating then suppressing then smothering
will it not go to the head?
Make you jittery?

Bloated with wealth and bombs collecting dust
your suit buttons about to pop
you squirm, itch to burst.
You ask my sisters and I to taste
your pearl-white power
entice you to come
teach our men how you do it
keeping the peace
then drink heartily afterwards
mercy showering our heads like the piss of a cherub.

I imagine the heart of the atom, the nucleus
warily watches us both.

At my core I am beautiful, she pleads,
my Strong Force electrifying.

Tempting, I know,
but should you disturb
bombard me with neutrons, I shall tear
and fission, burn like an angry angel
cauterize your civilizations.

You will lose small details
like how to feel chagrined
you may confuse flurries of ash
for snowflakes on a fawn
misplace your history books and never know
if your son takes after your father.

Which direction is downwind?
See the fallout boring into dirt
like splinters of mangled bone.

Perhaps it's best then for you
to starve some of my people.
Early were we seated at the table.
You could have raised your glass then
to a line by Jalal ad-Din Rumi, not bid us
chew on the lining of our mouths.

Like a watchdog you sit across the continent
rationing emaciated jaws
quantifying the generated power.

Now as I write, clutching his maroon
Allah-emblazoned passport
an Iranian father makes his way
to the Canadian border to wave at his son
the Niagara Horseshoe gushing between them,
effervescent in its welcome.

Native

The thermometer grazes one hundred at near dusk. I squint into
the heat and walk with a self-preserving pace to the trash bin,
past the native, deer-resistant California lilac I planted some springs ago.
It's almost fall and the lilac squats stunted, nibbled to three bare sticks.

I spot a lone doe in your yard, still as a taxidermy,
sustained by sparse poisonous shrubs, this golden landscape
of dearth. The hunger in her eyes, her commanding drive to survive,
I interpret in my wishful thinking into a reasonable effort,
nothing egregious I hope—Ranch dressing perhaps, not quite
poison, but the way my Persian palate accommodates, happily tolerates
the plastic squeak of julienned bell peppers, croutons in a salad.

Perhaps she rations poison akin to the measured gestures I mete out still
after all these years, to acclimate, address strangers with well-oiled
greetings in lines in coffee shops and farmers markets, beaming
under the shameless sun, in a baseball cap and cut-off shorts.

The truth is you'll be hard pressed to find fault with me.
Even now, neighbor, as we eye each other askance from across
the road, you itching to run me out, like the pest you would down
for foraging your dry lawn. I've grown decorously unselective, pasture
in pure reception, neither preference, nor denial. I imagine I'd be
crowned victor by now, at the ceremony of natural selection, a survivor
peering at you through brown gazelle eyes, virtually colorblind.

Next time a cousin visits and asks where I come from, you'll find
me embalmed, preserved as a curio. You may point. I'm a precious collector's
item. But for now, won't you come in for a drink, neighbor? I've minced
the barbed leaves, for want of black wild berries this year, you know
how they've shriveled like dark little clenched fists. I've snapped the dusty
sticks too from the brier, coarsely ground them into this *Blackberry Bramble*.

Let us toast and feel the draught rip our throats, hit the same gnawing
spot we share in this scorching twilight; it seems no ordinary drink will
wash away our animosity, each hunkering uninsured at home in the heart
of the *High Fire Hazard Severity Zone* where you stand and brandish your gun,
the American flag leaning to take a strike at the air beyond your deck.

The truth is I've grown weary of giving you no reason to shoot. What shame
that I too now listen to the breeze as though it rustled through the blue oaks
to spite me. I wish you'd play along, amiable as a tabula rasa, a still-life.

I go through my Monday rituals, fasting to remember the humiliation of hunger
and pour two drops of bleach on the lid of my fifty-gallon refuse bin to keep
the bears at bay, and retreat back inside. Two hours north, Tahoe residents
share their crawl space, what's called *bearbnb*. In Paradise, an hour
northeast, the homeless roam like ghosts, the ash refusing to settle.

Bared

The small phalanx has returned, bustling over dandelions. I put off
mowing for a third morning and listen. The sunny flowers give, tousled
under one bee then another, by noon they fold or go to seed.

I welcome the quiet in the wake of the bees—a lapse in the drone
of weed-whippers clearing dry brush, chain saws felling bone-
stripped ponderosas. Near and far, we make the air pulsate—

back-to-back from dawn till two, then again at sundown, we make room,
more defensible room for fire trucks, evacuation routes. I have plenty
of visibility now, the woods a manicured park of blue oaks. Naked up to

the waist, silky madronas peel before my eyes. I walk the dog, check on
toyon at the bend in the road. It came out in June, thick creamy clusters
quickly wilting like a bouquet in the musty hands of an anxious bride.

Now it hangs with waxy red berries dented black as tooth decay. To think
Hollywood received its name from this scrub, her spot-bald boughs
gracing centerpieces at Christmas. She could poultice a wound, soften

thirst, fresh or dried and ground, she would feed me, as she did the Muwekma
Ohlone, the American Robin, the mockingbird. with her pomes, her leaves
hesitant as a rose. She leans messy and fungus-ridden over the scotch-broom.

I've seen them take cover at these two brambles here: the hare transfixed
at their feet by the incoming headlight, the proud doe, too, the high priestess
of the woods wavers here at *Toyon,* the *Terminus,* the last remaining buffer

at the junction of two worlds. I walk back and down the driveway. Come nightfall,
creatures shall shiver like stars, stare unblinking into the blackness now bared
and leveled. I keep vigil—my home lit up loud as a blunder.

This Used to Be the Sea. One Day We Looked Out, We Couldn't See the Sea.

The mountain began disappearing in truckloads.
It was erected during the civil war—axiomatic proof
that wars do not cause dearth, but excess, not exactly abundance,
but sufficient dirt to add a mountain to the earth.

We called it Borj Hammoud Mountain, a soft yawn
of sentient slumber that knew our city's intimate
rhythms, our rapacious appetite and daily cleansing
rituals—the shedding of leftover errors and facts
as unbecoming as half-formed contaminated

children and mangled steel. It crawled with long snakes
and our meek beliefs in those Samaritan gestures
which were intended to add up in good time and absolve
the city of dross. And refrigerators, countless stainless

steel refrigerators that no longer preserved our dewy dreams
yet refused to thaw into the thin air of our expectations.
And we carried on with our seaside escapade, encased in
whitewashed Mediterranean walls adorned with azure tiles,

fortified illusions that couldn't keep the strident stench out.
It rammed itself into rooms, felt no need to ooze
beneath doors into basements, it appeared through sheer will.
While we waited patiently for a change in the direction of toxic
wind, we taught our children to inhale death in smaller sips.
Borj Hammoud Mountain—our communal black hole
of nondescript inequity, topped with dirt, a cat half covering
her dump, innocent enough. Then the mountain began disappearing.

A procession of trucks passed us daily, glowing with heavy metal, radioactive green, microplastic teeming with sluggish bacteria, a thin juice dripping at our doors. Accompanied at every round by its faithful flock of seagulls, the mountain was eventually expunged (though the rats remained like loyal pets), and we had reclaimed our natural land.

Then one numbered day, our fishermen returned with mad talk of scaled creatures floating on the sea like slaughter, of fetid screams that bubbled in pain and refused to lie on their sides.

And we awoke, one unconscionable morning, to find we had shoved the sea out of our way.

Shopping

Each time I prepare a list
I forget something ineffable—
the white wound of rubber

trees bleeding latex,
the vulnerability of roots in
a baby-six-pack of parsley plugs,
also plastic,

black and thinly
negligible. The cling to life
after death-on-the-stand
of fresh gills and the thrashing tail.

Each time I venture out
I take thinner sips of air,
weigh myself

against quality on the grand scale.
I buy time in aisle after bleach-lit
aisle, reading labels,

for the most cost-effective
way to squander.
Possibilities swarm

with beeswax and balsam.
Cultivars and colognes,
each contains an entire

terrain from Provence or
a close semblance. I sift through

my needs, sniff my wrists,
smile and mutter

an excuse to the salesperson
for why I cannot afford the air.

Even so, each time I leave, embracing
a package or two, I feel refurbished,
confident it will smooth over
like a coat of whitewash
or at least identify what is missing.

Listen! Who is crying?
I can barely hear it anymore.

Eggplants

In a sun-soaked spot in the garden,
half-veiled by broad purple-veined leaves,
Black Beauties dangle,

burying bare heads
in the warmth
of a late summer bed.

*

Did the eggplants
back home,
potbellied and turgid,
dangle different?

Different from the Sicilians
or the heirloom Fairy Tales?

Remember how we stood
them in rows on the kitchen counter
like mothers in queues
of Tehran-Bazaar, wrapped
from head to toe in black chadors?

*

Yet for all their protection in yards
and yards of tough patent leather sheen,
the eggplants back home collapsed into a pile
of slush in less than an hour in the oven.

It must have to do with the loamy soil.

*

In my palm, the petite Fairy Tale is far
from a shade of night.

It's covered in neat streaks of white light
like well-managed shooting stars.

I suspect it has issues.
Refuses to yield much seed
lest it bloat and bitter.

Eschews color too.

Watch me and learn, it says,
Sweetness is promised in your name,
not in the well-conditioned soil.

Live up to your name!
All of you, go on, grow!
Be fruitful!

*

Little Fingers is more reserved.
Less need be said
when you are the origin of things.

It's pendulous, suspended from the calyx—
a drop of ink holding dark
to history.

Run your fingers
down the bruised body to the head.
Its firm flesh ends in awe.

Not as in cucumbers
bolting like children into lanky limbs,
but the father, tender in his prime.

*

Between Ichiban and Tycoon,
between Rosa Bianca and Violetta di Firenze,
between Louisiana Long Green and Thai Green,

Black Beauty bows
under the California sun,
sending her roots into the red
sere clay of the Sierra foothills.

*

IV

A Muslim

I get the news from my deaf mother
on FaceTime, my 2008 MacBook air her portal
to the maze beyond her rented basement flat
in Clovis—the home of GMO agriculture—
where asthma or another respiratory ailment
knocks at every childbearing household
by a toddler's third birthday, demanding ransom
or sometimes an outright sacrifice.

My mother keeps windows shut
in all seasons, her nose runs regardless.
She signs in annoyance and tucks the tissue
down one sleeve. It took weeks to teach her arthritic
finger to single, not double tap the touchpad.
You need to learn to read the alphabet, I repeat.
She attends ASL lessons, she insists, and follows
her Mexican friends just fine. I keep passwords
to six times zero and coax her away from sites
insistent on special characters. But the truth is
she is better off here, navigating her two tabs,
not guzzling exhaust on the lookout for Tehran's
Morality Police. She scrolls, *likes* and shares
on Facebook like a child and totters along
on Persian BBC with grade school literacy.
We communicate with bare essentials, omit verbs,
prepositions, clauses, we stick to the truth.

Today she tells me,

Three hundred, blown up.

Her arms briefly vanish from the screen.

I've heard, I sign.

S-R-I-L-A-N-K-A!

She tags each guttural sound to the next,
eight letters detonating in midair
and I am that embarrassed child
again who'd tug and tug at a hem
till she'd lowered her voice.

I say, *It's close to India.*

دلم میسوزه
My heart is burning,

she signs, her face sorry as though she
were somehow culpable. Then she asks
the question I've felt coming all along.
And since I have no Farsi words to spare

for a *terrorist,*
a militant Islamist
a Religious Extremist,
or an *ISIS member,*

I carefully construct the truth in my mind:

Eight Muslims wrapped each other in explosives
and blew up two hundred fifty-nine Christians

in retaliation for one Christian
who blasted fifty Muslims last month,

feeling an odd pinch of pride in my precision of language.

But I look into the expectant face,
grateful I cannot recall the Farsi word, and float *Fifi*
groomed and fluffy before the screen.

My mother's lined face breaks into a brief smile.

    On skype, your aunt says there is no rice, she signs,
    no bread back home,
    the north flooded,
    the sky, land, and sea inseparable.

دلم میسوزه.

Quince

This April, blossoms weigh on the quince,
its slender arms covered in volutes about to break
into hives once the rains should pass. Last fall,
I drove five hours to Clovis and dropped my harvest

of seven at my mother's door. They'd peaked,
past posing on the mantle for a still-life, their perfume
still a head-turner like a woman cresting, her prime
soon behind her. *Amoo* always kept to a few objects,

the blue adobe jar, its rippled mouth hardest
to render, and a pome fruit, a medlar or two, their spears
in a tangle, but when the quince arrived in the market,
we transported the Mallorca platter to the studio

and I, the young assistant, stood sentinel as he balanced
each fruit on thumb and two fingers, careful with the dreamy
fuzz on the golden skin, he tipped and tilted till the light
bared the most fetching profile, and one by one, pressing

their hips into each other they sat, blossom-ends up,
and where the flesh dimpled, where the severed stalk still held
to a last leaf, he left ample room, for in a moment, the breeze
would enter and pass through the arrangement in praise.

Siavash

for my father

Could he have uttered a word
    at all he would've cooed into my ear
like a rock dove, his mouth a clipped
    wing, my maimed altar of worship.

He would have risen with the gurgle
    of the radiator at dawn, with the first call
to prayer, he would've known the clamor
    of his tools, heard the chatter

of the handsaw, baby teeth nibbling through
    poplar slabs, *glissando, glissando.*
It should have been him
    who heard the sorrel that raised a storm of red

sweeping John Wayne across Monument
    Valley. He should have heard the cowboy dubbed
into Farsi on our brand-new color TV, the travail
    of that thoroughbred, he was in love

with its bridled throat, un-winded like his own—
    his breath only just audible in the absolute silence
that corralled him in, led him out and into rooms.
    He should have heard our pale old Peykan,

I couldn't tell what ailed it. It lamented of winter
    but how was I to sign a car chugging, sighing
to a stall into his eyes? It would shiver unwilling
    to mount the on-ramp of Seyed Khandan.

My father, you were a child of ten.
    Did you know the purpose
of that pilgrimage to Mashhad? They pressed
    your head against the shrine, you slept

through the starless night, your slight ankles
    fettered to the steely luster of the latticed
window. The autumn equinox was burdened,
    burdened with rounds of surahs that night.

At daybreak Khanoom joon and Mamman joon
    broke vigil, chadors slipping
to their shoulders they whispered:

                    Siavash!

                            Siavash, Siavash!

Into your ear, against the morning breeze
they called your name,

                    Siavash!

The matron saint kept deaf as steel to their pleas
though the two women
would've laid their lives at her feet
to awaken the dead drums of your ears.

Beloved

I see now that all is well—the black mission,
prolific, fruit spaced out three inches along
each limb, the cat drops off a mole a day,
never a bird; a flock of house finches fret
on the weed-ridden lawn as though dandelions
were at stake. This is how I think it victory,
looking back at that final visit to *Parioli*.
Around our usual corner on the elegant *via Collina*,
graffiti now screamed in red and green,

Stranieri! Leave and leave Italy for Italians!

We queued at the *Alimentari* for a bottle
of *ferrarelle naturale* and a block of *Bel Paese*,
you clutching your cane, the MSF contact
for physician-assisted suicide face down
in your drawer like a wild card.
This is how I loved you—calling on *la Signora*
from behind his lavish display case, the clerk
skipped us and you went on leaning into that grand
ivory handle, your brow lifted under that invisible
crown of laurels as if in that moment the very world
had need of us, and I pressed the heels
of my patent leather stilettos into my spot in line,
lifted my diminutive head in genteel
admiration of the animated flourish
of the bow of a *panettone* before me.

Yes, we abided as though we belonged,
with our painstakingly-acquired palate
for fine cheese. Thirsty for the expensive
effervescence of spring water we stood

with just enough euros in our pockets
for a final ration of water and a wedge
of *Bel Paese*—the glamorous country
you had courted and escorted me through.

Your love affair of a lifetime! *Italia!*
where I too learned to woo. Seduced by the lilt
of her tongue, I tagged along, ran ahead
careening the rounded corners of her cobbled alleys.
Her carefree cadence rolled off the soft palate
of your mouth and nestled into my ears, language
gushing at windblown fountains where gods
coupled in the open, where I, the lovestruck child,
raised my pinwheel to ride the same generous wind.

You poured her like pearls onto my lap as though
she were yours to bequeath—this country that now
shrugged you off as you made ready to die, frightened
the night would come where you would need
ask of her to raise your head for a sip of water.

The Italian Civil State Office and the Iranian Embassy Deny Your Request for Cremation

For ten years now I have found
                 comfort in the freshness
                 of the one droplet on your corpse
clinging like morning dew
                 to your right cheek, refusing to roll. A tear
would have—that much is certain. The mortician,
a public servant of Rome, left the room
with his tired eyes, your shirt and tie
                 neatly stacked,
and the pressed suit. Your socks and briefs, I handed
to him on his return. On the last trip he took the bouquet
                 from my hand, and your shoes. I ask
myself, *the cut roses, were they not crisp*
the next morning? They lay stiffly on the bed
of baby's breath when I returned
the next morning. Stems caught
                 in your cuffs, they reached
                 with clean white faces for your chin. I saw
well enough, I spotted the single droplet
                 on your cheek, you see, through the grease
                 of fingerprints at eye level. The sweaty
plexiglass pane stretched uninterrupted
from cold stony floor
to ceiling. My love, you were
                 seamlessly sealed
away for good. *Yes,*
all is good, I tell myself, *at museums too, a thermostat*
regulates the ambient temperature. I tell myself,
                 public morgues are kept perpetually chilled,
                 cold and clean as holy mountains.
                 And the high-pressured hose—

no doubt he must have

           circled you clockwise

or not, no matter, three times

to be sure, mercy raining

           down hard, long

enough to pool about the drain. I swear,

           the dewdrop on your face

my witness. Then the spray of baby's breath, the roses

may rest easy. Surely, he must have

rolled you onto your side,

on the stainless-steel

           gurney, an assistant,

likely a lean teenage lad had wielded

the unruly hose.

           Did the stream follow the gnarled,

           sinuous path through the ravine years of care

           had carved into the blades

of your back? I could have

assured him

           they were whittled

down in love. I could have shown him where

           to linger, let the water

linger over varicosed calves,

           over a gentle soul.

*

Does his girlfriend now wear

the knotted silver ring you never

           once pulled off that baby finger?

In ten days, you arrived at San Francisco

Airport, barely embalmed, bloated,

           foaming, putrid in the coffin.

           My love, I signed

what papers they put before me.

The next morning a breeze

swept in across the bar. I watched it lean
the white sails toward starboard and lift
your heavy ashes
into the air. By Angel Island I scattered after you
my armful of red
roses into blue.

My Only Bangle

for Khanoom joon, my great-grandmother

after Lucille Clifton

Today I celebrate my only bangle
my one-hand applause
the gold leaf on my family tree
my hand-hammered heritage
my blood.
Today it refused
to slide off, a rounded portal
barring my hand
in spite of the sweet-talking soap
the slip of cold cream
in spite of not matching
my low-cut cocktail dress, my silver choker.
It cleaved to knuckle and bone
held me by the wrist
each unalloyed carat ablaze —
Here, it whispered, *rub some kohl*
under your eyes before you step out,
then let me hear you
pronounce your name.

Notes

Most poems in this collection were inspired by the art of my uncle Bahman Mohassess (1931-2010). Please visit my website to view the corresponding collages that prompted individual poems.

The title "Death Was Like a Desire" quotes an anonymous woman who was imprisoned in the Evin prison in Tehran.

The title "They Were Blind and Mad, Some of Them Were Laughing. There Was Nobody to Lead the Blind People." borrows the words of Bahar Ahmed as she is quoted in the article "We Blame Saddam for Everything," published in *The Guardian* on March 17, 2003.

"Khorramshahr, 1980" is in response to the tragic fate of Mohammad Hossein Fahmideh who is celebrated as a war hero by the government of the Islamic Republic of Iran. Mohammad left for the frontlines at the age of thirteen and wrapped in explosives threw himself under an Iraqi tank. His suicide on November 10, 1980 was the decisive moment which forced the Iraqi troops to retreat in the Battle of Khorramshahr.

The italicized line in "Believers" quotes Surah *Al-Baqarah*, Ayat 18, in the Qur'an.

"Intoxicated by Verses:" In Moslem theology the Qur'an should always be recited in Arabic, not in translation.

"Sparkling like the stars above" in "Childhood" is borrowed from the lyrics of "Romeo and Juliet" by Dire Straits.

"This Used to Be the Sea. One Day We Looked Out, We Couldn't See the Sea" addresses Lebanon's waste management crisis which remains unresolved today, affecting the ecosystem and the health of the population. The title quotes Arpi Kruzian in the Reuters article, "No End to Crisis in Sight as Lebanon's Garbage Mountains Grow," by Ellen Francis, dated February 4, 2018.

"A Muslim" is in response to the tragic events of Easter Sunday, April 21, 2019. Three churches in Sri Lanka and three luxury hotels in the commercial capital Colombo were targeted in a series of coordinated terrorist suicide bombings.

The italicized lines in "When Your Sky Runs Into Mine" are from Act III, Scene 1 of *The Merchant of Venice* by William Shakespeare.

President Trump's travel ban affected many ordinary citizens' lives. "Sanctions" came as a response to an NPR news story where being denied entry into the United States to visit his son, a father travels to Horseshoe Falls in Ontario, Canada. Father and son wave at each other from across the Niagara waterfall.

Acknowledgements

Many thanks to the editors of the following journals where these poems first appeared, at times in earlier versions and under different titles.

Cream City Review: "Iran Politics in First Grade," "Spared"

The Rumpus: "Before and After the Revolution," "Mrs. Farahmand and Mrs. Henderson Share Drinks on the Eve of War," "The Italian Civil State Office and the Iranian Embassy Deny Your Request for Cremation"

Narrative Magazine: "They Were Blind and Mad, Some of Them Were Laughing. There Was Nobody to Lead the Blind People.," "Khorramshahr, 1980," "The Immigrant and Skin," "Death Was Like a Desire"

New Letters: "War of the Cities"

Southern Humanities Review: "War," "Believers"

CALYX Journal: "Ramazan in Tajrish," "My Only Bangle"

Poetry Northwest: "Madar"

RHINO Poetry: "By Age Ten I Understood the Heft of Fabrics"

The Ekphrastic Review: "Intoxicated by Verses," "Silence"

Potomac Review: "Straniera"

Ninth Letter: "First Kiss"

Poet Lore: "Childhood"

San Pedro River Review: "At Twelve"

Artemis: "Magnolia Grandiflora"

The Florida Review: "Loneliness"

The Woven Tale Press: "Shopping"

Tuck Magazine: "This Used to Be the Sea. One Day We Looked Out, We Couldn't See the Sea."

The Bare Life Review: "Eggplants"

The Pinch: "A Muslim"

International Literary Quarterly: "Sky and Sea," "Native"

Native Skin: "Interview for Asylum"

California Fire & Water: A Climate Crisis Anthology: "Bared"

"Intoxicated by Verses" was reprinted in *The Dewdrop* in 2022.

With gratitude to Shara McCallum for her abounding generosity. Ellen Bass, thank you for lending me your stamina in this art. Gratitude to Kwame Dawes whose vision shaped these poems into a book manuscript. Gratitude to my companions-in-art for being there: Allison Moore, Allisa Cherry, Carrie Beyer, Emily Tobias, James Ryder, Rhony Bopla, Jeanne Yu, Eliza, Tudor, Thea Swanson, Beatriz Brenes, Ruth Atkins, John DeMarco, Jo Anna Mortenson, Agnes Cartry, Ana Michalowsky, Judith Grace, Stefano Petrizzo, and Claire Walker. I thank the MacDowell Fellowship for the generous support which allowed me to put the final touches to this manuscript in the tranquil setting of the woods of New Hampshire. Thank you, Esther Lee and the team at Elixir Press for your care and attention with this collection. Thank you, Tangkao, for your support, always. And finally, with love for my family in Iran and the US. Fariba, Siavash, Leyla, Sara, and Nima, this book is for you and for our departed loved ones.

ELIXIR PRESS TITLES

POETRY TITLES

Circassian Girl by Michelle Mitchell-Foust
Imago Mundi by Michelle Mitchell-Foust
Distance From Birth by Tracy Philpot
Original White Animals by Tracy Philpot
Flow Blue by Sarah Kennedy
A Witch's Dictionary by Sarah Kennedy
The Gold Thread by Sarah Kennedy
Rapture by Sarah Kennedy
Monster Zero by Jay Snodgrass
Drag by Duriel E. Harris
Running the Voodoo Down by Jim McGarrah
Assignation at Vanishing Point by Jane
    Satterfield
Her Familiars by Jane Satterfield
The Jewish Fake Book by Sima Rabinowitz
Recital by Samn Stockwell
Murder Ballads by Jake Adam York
Floating Girl (Angel of War) by Robert
    Randolph
Puritan Spectacle by Robert Strong
X-testaments by Karen Zealand
Keeping the Tigers Behind Us by Glenn J.
    Freeman
Bonneville by Jenny Mueller
State Park by Jenny Mueller
Cities of Flesh and the Dead by Diann Blakely
Green Ink Wings by Sherre Myers
Orange Reminds You Of Listening by Kristin
    Abraham
*In What I Have Done & What I Have Failed To
    Do* by Joseph P. Wood
Bray by Paul Gibbons
The Halo Rule by Teresa Leo
Perpetual Care by Katie Cappello
*The Raindrop's Gospel: The Trials of St. Jerome
    and St. Paula* by Maurya Simon
Prelude to Air from Water by Sandy Florian

Let Me Open You A Swan by Deborah Bogen
Cargo by Kristin Kelly
Spit by Esther Lee
Rag & Bone by Kathryn Nuerenberger
Kingdom of Throat-stuck Luck by George
    Kalamaras
Mormon Boy by Seth Brady Tucker
Nostalgia for the Criminal Past by Kathleen
    Winter
I will not kick my friends by Kathleen Winter
Little Oblivion by Susan Allspaw
Quelled Communiqués by Chloe Joan Lopez
Stupor by David Ray Vance
Curio by John A. Nieves
The Rub by Ariana-Sophia Kartsonis
Visiting Indira Gandhi's Palmist by Kirun Kapur
Freaked by Liz Robbins
Looming by Jennifer Franklin
Flammable Matter by Jacob Victorine
Prayer Book of the Anxious by Josephine Yu
flicker by Lisa Bickmore
Sure Extinction by John Estes
Selected Proverbs by Michael Cryer
Rise and Fall of the Lesser Sun Gods by Bruce
    Bond
Barnburner by Erin Hoover
Live from the Mood Board by Candice Reffe
Deed by Justin Wymer
Somewhere to Go by Laurin Becker Macios
*If We Had a Lemon We'd Throw It and Call
    That the Sun* by Christopher Citro
White Chick by Nancy Keating
The Drowning House by John Sibley Williams
Green Burial by Derek Graf
When Your Sky Runs into Mine by Rooja
    Mohassessy
Degrees of Romance by Peter Krumbach

FICTION TITLES

How Things Break by Kerala Goodkin
Juju by Judy Moffat
Grass by Sean Aden Lovelace
Hymn of Ash by George Looney
The Worst May Be Over by George Looney
Nine Ten Again by Phil Condon
Memory Sickness by Phong Nguyen
Troglodyte by Tracy DeBrincat

The Loss of All Lost Things by Amina Gautier
The Killer's Dog by Gary Fincke
Everyone Was There by Anthony Varallo
The Wolf Tone by Christy Stillwell
Tell Me, Signora by Ann Harleman
Far West by Ron Tanner
Out of Season by Kirk Wilson
The Paper Anniversary by Dinah Cox